An Invitation to Tea

This book was printed in the United States of America.

To order additional copies of this book, contact:
Xlibris Corporation
1-888-795-4274
www.Xlibris.com
Orders@Xlibris.com

INTRODUCTION... *5*

CHAPTER ONE... *7*
Occasions for Tea

CHAPTER TWO... *11*
Getting Started

CHAPTER THREE... *16*
Table Presentation

CHAPTER FOUR... *29*
Menu

CHAPTER FIVE... *49*
All About Tea

CHAPTER SIX... *59*
Children's Teas

CHAPTER SEVEN... *62*
Frequently Asked Questions

INTRODUCTION

What is Afternoon Tea?

Afternoon Tea is a time of quiet reflection.

It is a gathering of tea lovers who wish to get together and share some titillating conversation amidst an abundance of lace, fresh flowers and fine bone china.

It is a calming time; a time to put on your finest dress and large floppy hat; a time to put the troubles of this crazy world on the shelf and go back to a more genteel way of life.

It is savoring the flavors of tiny finger sandwiches, freshly baked scones with lashings of lemon curd and luscious Devonshire cream. It is delicate bite-sized pastries and confections. It is piping hot tea, perfectly brewed and served in sparkling silver teapots.

It is fun, laughter and rejoicing. It is all of these things and more.

It is a special time.

CHAPTER ONE
Occasions for Tea

Any occasion to bring a friend or two together is a good thing, and what better way to achieve this than to host an afternoon tea in the comfort of your own home? It's a familiar place and your invited guests will feel comfortable there. Create a reason to gather your nearest and dearest of old friends (or brand new ones), and you are well on the way to presenting your own afternoon tea.

Some reasons may be obvious; a birthday, anniversary or bridal shower. But there are many times when no special event is needed; getting together the first of the month to catch up on local gossip, or having a tea after a book club/church group/card game meeting. Celebrating the first day of spring (or the last day of winter), or in support of someone going through a tough patch in their life. Welcoming a new home, a new job, new baby, or for just because . . . . . . there really doesn't have to be a special reason.

The important thing to remember is that you've taken the time to share of yourself with those you care about. Long after they have experienced your tea and hospitality, your friends will be sure to remember you, the laughter, and the sharing of good times, but will have long forgotten the initial reason for visiting you in the first place.

Tea Venues

Once you have determined the occasion for your tea, you are ready to decide on where in your home to present it.

A home doesn't have to be large in order to host a tea, and you don't have to confine it to just one room. The dining room is an obvious first choice, but if you are not able to seat everyone around your table, then by all means, spread out to other adjoining rooms by adding a series of card tables for example. Once the tables are decorated, your home will look more like a quaint tea room and will give added charm to your party.

Alternatively, you could present your tea as a buffet. Buffets are often a first choice for larger groups of people and are less formal than a sit down tea. In this instance a central location serves as the food station, and the guests come to it and help themselves. The chosen area should have good traffic flow and be easy to access. If you have an island or largish counter space in the kitchen, this would work well. Or maybe a kitchen table could be utilized. The actual dining room table can be used as a buffet and once the chairs have been removed, it is an ideal place to showcase your tea items.

Once your guests have chosen their food items, they can mix and mingle with others, find a comfy place to sit, placing their plates and cups on end tables, coffee tables, or even window ledges if they wish. You should make sure that prior to your tea, you have cleared enough space for them to do this.

Weather permitting, a garden tea can be a most delightful experience. We have all seen images of a lace-covered table complete with pretty teacups, dainty sandwiches and scones dripping with cream and strawberry jam – all set amid a beautiful English cottage garden. The majority of us may not have a cottage garden complete with rose-covered arbors, but we can certainly replicate the English tea table very easily.

As lovely as all this sounds, make sure you don't have uninvited guests of the insect variety come join in the fun! Nothing can be more annoying than wasps, ants and mosquitoes honing in on your special tea. If your bug problem is minor, you may be able to control it with various remedies from your local hardware store. But, if you have a real issue with these pesky creatures, you may be better to host your tea party indoors.

Also, be mindful of the heat and humidity. Not only will your guests wilt in high temperatures, it's also not a good idea to have potentially hazardous food items (cream, milk, protein-rich foods, etc.) sitting outside in the warm sunshine for fear of food-borne illness developing. Your guests will want to remember your tea party for the wonderful experience it was, not for the tummy bug that plagued them the next day.

And no matter where you decide to ultimately hold your tea, always have plan "B" on the drawing board. Perfect weather is never a certainty when you would like it to be, so be prepared to move the whole event under cover, in a hurry, if necessary. A carefully planned tea is a happy tea for all concerned.

CHAPTER TWO
Getting Started

Invitations

The first order of the day is to let your invited guests know they're invited! You could call or email them, but that would be so impersonal. The best and most gracious way is to send out a handwritten invitation.

Invitations can be anything from simple, pretty cards to elaborate gold embossed affairs. It really doesn't matter which kind you choose as long as the pertinent information is included.

Maybe you have a theme in mind, in which case you could try and find cards that suit the idea. Failing that, you could make your own. Craft stores have an abundance of supplies to get those creative juices flowing, and there are plenty of salespersons on hand who will guide you to what you need.

To get you started, I have listed a few examples. Once you begin, I am confident you will come up with many more ideas of your own. Remember, the invites don't have to be perfect. It is the message that is important, not your artwork. Believe me, your chosen guests will be duly impressed that you took the time to create your own, unique invitations and will eagerly await your special tea party on the chosen day.

Take a simple card stock (plain or pastel shade is best), and cut it to the size you would like it to be. A finished 4"x6" folded card would be a good size, making sure you are able to find envelopes to match. Depending on your theme, use decorative stickers (scrap-booking stores have a wealth of ideas), cut out photographs of your theme topic, and then add small ribbon bows or buttons. You could even glue tiny, reasonably flat silk flowers to the front. If your tea is a celebration for a particular person, cut out a photo of the special guest and glue that to the front of the card. Add the words, "You're Invited to Tea" with a felt-tip marker, paints, or stencil the letters and your invitation is nearly complete.

Alternatively, you could find a photo of a cup or teapot and enlarge it to the size of the invitation. Then carefully trace around the edge on to card stock and cut out the shape. Remember to fold it in half first. This shape then becomes your actual invitation. Add a decorative design with your own personal touch and you have another unique way of inviting your guests to tea.

To add a really different angle to your invitation, take a glue pen and write the words, "You're Invited to Tea". Quickly sprinkle real, unused tea leaves on the wet glue. Shake off any excess and let completely dry for at least 30 minutes. If you use a particularly aromatic tea (Earl Grey, Jasmine or any flavored tea), not only will your invitation be decorative, it will smell wonderful too!

Whatever kind of invitation you decide to use, it is very important that the inside message answer the five "w's" – What, Why, When, Who and Where?

For example:

> What? Please come to an afternoon tea
> Why? Give reason for tea gathering (Jane's birthday, Susie's bridal shower, etc.)
> When? Date and time of tea
> Who? Hosted by (your name)
> Where? Your address and telephone number
> R.S.V.P. Ask guests to respond by a certain date

Add any additional instructions you feel will be helpful, like specific driving directions, or whether your guests should wear hats or gloves. If this tea is intended to be a celebration for someone special, clearly state whether it is intended to be a surprise or not. You would hate to go to all the trouble of keeping it a secret, only to find out the guest of honor knows all about it before she even arrives!

Send off your invitations in plenty of time (two or three weeks before your tea), and have the R.S.V.P.'s returned a week before to give you plenty of time to make adjustments to your menu. Invariably, there will be someone who either forgets to respond, or doesn't think she has to and you will be chasing her down by telephone for her commitment. At least if you have a week in hand, you will be able to find the time to take care of this and other minor problems.

Please Come to a Tea Party
For the Garden Club's
10th Anniversary

Sunday, June 1st, 2009
At 12:30 p.m.

Hosted by
Denise Whipple
In her garden
(Weather permitting)

27, St. Mary's Avenue
Clarkston, MI 48346

248-625-8911

Kindly RSVP by May 24th
And please wear a floppy hat!

A Garden Tea Invitation

An example showing the front of the invitation and suggested information for the inside

A Few Dos and Don'ts about Receiving Invitations

There are certain protocols which need to be followed if you are lucky enough to have received an invitation.

- Always respond promptly with your reply, either by telephone or mail, especially if there is a specific R.S.V.P. included.

- Never assume it is ok to bring along another guest who was not invited (and this includes children and pets). It is equally rude to ask your host if you may do so.

- If you have to decline an invitation because of a house guest, it is perfectly correct to inform your host that this is the reason you are regretfully unable to attend. Only if your host then suggests including your houseguest is it alright to do so.

- Alert your host to any food allergies you may have, but do not expect a complete change of menu. She will then be sure to include enough of a selection of food items from which you may choose.

- On the day of the tea arrive at the appointed time, or even a few minutes early to ensure the event can start promptly. If the tea is in an unfamiliar area, check the mileage and route and give yourself plenty of time to arrive at your destination. Allow for inclement weather and time of day. These and other traffic factors may impact your travel time.

- It is considered courteous to arrive at the tea with a small token gift for the host. This can be some flowers or maybe a tea-related item. Your host is not expected to use or display your gift that day, so do not be disappointed if you don't see your beautiful arrangement of tea roses as the main centerpiece. In all probability, the decorations have previously been arranged to match the host's table. If this is the case, a gracious host will thank you for your thoughtfulness and place the arrangement in another part of the room to enjoy later.

- Do call the next day to thank your host for a lovely tea party. An additional hand-written note of appreciation is always welcome and is a nice keepsake for the host to have.

CHAPTER THREE
Table Presentation

If your dining room table doesn't have six leaves, bringing it to a grand length of fifteen feet, don't worry. In fact, don't worry if your table is only of the coffee variety. Afternoon tea is flexible enough to be served on whatever you have on hand. It's the perfect way to entertain because there are no set rules.

Tables come in many shapes, styles and sizes, and all will work beautifully for your tea party. With a little imagination and time, your tea table will transform itself into a work of art.

However, to enhance the appearance of an ordinary looking table, it is first necessary to cover it with your best linens. The use of linens and napkins is known as "napery".

A Little Napery History

In Roman times, dinner guests around the table would actually use the tablecloth as a napkin!

Later, in medieval years, messy eating habits meant messy cloths. So, the table used to be layered with several tablecloths, and when a spill occurred, the dirty cloth was removed, leaving a clean one underneath. Proper linen cloths also denoted rank or status and were very important in making an impression.

The Victorians also used layered cloths for the same purpose, but they were known as "accidental cloths". Depending on what was served, by the time dessert arrived the cloths had sometimes all been used and discarded leaving a bare table!

The prettiest of tables can have many layers of fine lace adorning them, but an inexpensive lacy-looking cloth will work just as well. Table runners can also be placed over a plain white tablecloth to give a more formal look to your table.

Whatever covering you choose to use, always remember the three C's: Crisp, Clean, Colorful and Coordinated.

Crisp:

The linens need to be ironed and pressed. There is nothing worse than a wrinkled tablecloth, and no matter what goes on top of it, the wrinkles will still show through. Creases, however, are inevitable and are quite acceptable. In fact, in the 17th and 18th Century it was very fashionable to have creases in the linens, and the host went to great lengths to achieve this look.

Clean:

It goes without saying that your tablecloths should be free of tears or marks of any kind. The china you use should also be inspected for old tea stains, or more importantly, lipstick marks left from a previous user. Silver or china teapots should sparkle and flatware should be polished with a clean cloth to remove any water marks. Milk jugs, sugar bowls and other condiment containers should also pass through the same rigid inspection.

Colorful:

The variety of your china teacups, saucers and plates placed on your table will immediately add color, but it will also be the three-tiered plate-stands or floral centerpieces that will set the scene. There are many ways to introduce color on to your table. If you have chosen pastel shades for your tea party, mix and match a variety of gentle colors together, possibly with pastel candles or single flowers at each guest's place. If your theme involves bolder, brighter colors, keep to those vibrant shades.

Coordinated:

This just means pulling everything together, and cloth napkins which compliment the color of the silk or fresh flowers is just one way to achieve this. Stand back and study your table as you would a work of art. Imagine a frame around the outside. Does it need a splash of pink there, or a dash of blue there? Is it balanced as regards height and space between the food stands and the centerpieces? Is your table overcrowded? Is the lighting too bright or too low?

You will soon learn what is pleasing to your eye and be able to create a "wow" table for your appreciative guests. It just takes a little practice and attention to those small, but very important details.

A Word about Napkins

Add elegance by keeping it simple and choosing napkin colors to match your décor or theme. There are many ways to fold your napkins, and a few of the popular ones are illustrated here. An attractive napkin fold adds that extra special detail to your table, plus your guests will be impressed by your expertise. If you are unable to achieve the illustrated folds, by all means simply fold the napkin in half and then into threes (like a brochure), and place it on the plate. This will look equally as elegant.

Some More Napkin History:

Over the years, the napkin has been worn over the arm, on the shoulder, or has been tied around the neck. Sometimes, fashion has hindered this latter activity. In Elizabethan times for instance, the large ruffled collars used to prevent the tying of the napkin in this way. This led to the saying, "having a hard time making ends meet".

The Goblet Fan

1 2 3 4

Lady Windermere's Fan

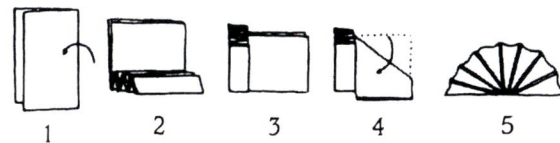

1 2 3 4 5

Pyramid

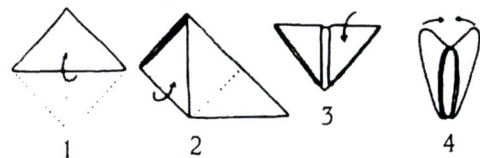

1 2 3 4

Diagrams courtesy of Gordon Food Service

Seated Tea

With a seated tea, guests are assigned a specific place to sit at your table. The food will be displayed either on three-tiered plate stands or on a series of raised plates and the guests help themselves as they wish.

Try not to crowd too many people around the table. Your guests will need elbow room and breathing space. If necessary, it will be better to set up another small table next to the larger one so guests are still able to converse with one another. If space is limited and this is not possible, by all means place another smaller table in another room, but make sure there are at least four people assigned to this additional table to ensure good company and conversation.

First, choose a white cloth that adequately fits the table and has at least a 12-18" overhang all around it. If the tea is to be a formal affair, then the cloth should be full length to the floor. Layer the look by adding a lacy or prettily embroidered over cloth. If you don't have one of these, you could overlap a series of smaller ones diagonally down the center of the table. These add interest to the table and form a focal point on which to build the rest of your tea table. Be imaginative and create your own special look. There are no hard and fast rules. Use whatever you have on hand to dress up your table.

Depending on how long the table is and how many guests are seated around it, will determine how many three-tiered stands (or food stations) are needed. I usually allow one stand per four persons. Therefore, a table of six to eight would require two stands, and between eight and twelve would require three to four stands. Every situation is different, but primarily you are trying to avoid overcrowding the plates with food, and at the same time, provide your guests easy access. Nobody should have to reach over somebody else to get to the goodies.

In the absence of three-tiered stands, which add height and decorative interest to the table, try to place individual food service plates on a riser of some kind rather than placing them flatly on the table. A riser could simply be a box covered with a lace cloth or napkin. Use different heights to give your table some depth.

Each individual place setting should comprise of a small plate centered in front of the guest. The napkin should rest in the center of this plate. A cup and saucer should be placed at the "2 o'clock" position with a small spoon sitting in the saucer on the right of the cup. The handle of the tea cup should be at the "4 o'clock" position. A knife, with the blade facing in, should be to the right of the plate. You probably don't need a fork, but if you wish to put one on the table, it should be to the left of the plate.

Centerpieces

In between these plate stands should be some kind of centerpiece. This could be as simple as freshly cut flowers placed in an old teapot, or smaller flowers, like tea roses, placed into some pretty teacups. A variety of decorative glass or china vases filled with flowers are also a perfect way to enhance the overall look.

If you own a glorious silver candelabra, this would certainly be the time to show it off. Sometimes, the more elaborate models come with a floral center area where you are able to add your own fresh arrangement. Another idea that was very popular in the Victorian times was to display brightly colored fruit on a risen pedestal. This centerpiece often contained flowers too, making it a spectacular table decoration.

If you don't wish to buy fresh flowers there are many alternatives. One simple idea I have used many times is a decorated hat stand with straw hat. Visit your local craft store and purchase a wrought-iron candle stand, a miniature plain straw hat and some pretty ribbons and silk flowers which match your other table decorations. Use the candle stand as the base and then decorate the straw hat by adding the ribbons and flowers, holding them in place with hot glue from a glue gun. Place the finished hat at an angle over the candle stand and voila! The perfect centerpiece. The overall effect is very charming and will fit the theme of many an afternoon tea.

Menu Cards

The addition of personal menu cards for each guest will definitely add a formal touch to your table.

If you are a dab hand at calligraphy, then by all means carefully write out each menu on a decoratively edged card. If this is not your forté, then the computer can certainly help you. There are many software programs available designed to produce everything from invites to thank you cards. Alternatively, print out the menu in a Word document. Add a silk flower (use that invaluable glue gun again), to the corner of the printed menu card and you have produced a special addition to your tea table.

Whichever method you choose, your menu card should be clearly displayed at the top of the place setting, facing the guest.

Celebration Bridal Tea

Sandwiches
Curried Egg Salad
Chicken, Walnut & Cranberry
Cucumber Dill

Scones
Sticky Cherry & Golden Raisin
Served with Devonshire Cream,
Strawberry Jam and Lemon Curd

Pastries
Fresh Fruit Tartlets   Pecan Diamonds
Apricot Fingers   Chocolate Truffles
Key Lime Tartlets   Lemon Gems
Chocolate-dipped Strawberries

Tea
Two Red Fruits
Darjeeling

Example of a Menu Card

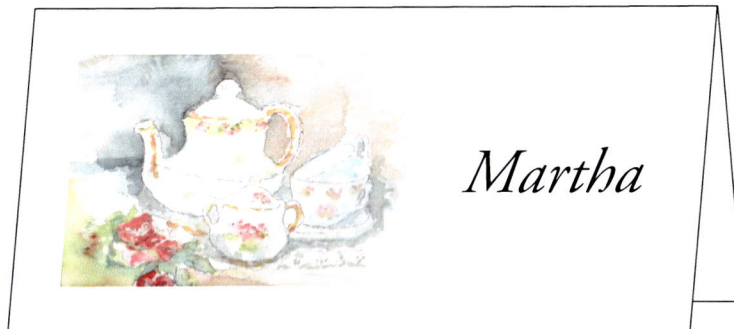

Martha

Place Cards

The use of place cards identify to your guests where they should be seated. They are very helpful, especially when dealing with a larger crowd, and can help to avoid confusion.

Place cards are often coordinated with menu cards in the way of matching decoration and design. For example, if you have decided to hand write the menu card, you should continue the theme and hand write each guest's name on the place card too.

The position of the place card is usually at the head of the place setting, just in front of the menu card. It can also sit on the center of the plate (if the napkin has been placed elsewhere, i.e. in a water glass or on the right of the place setting). Wherever the place card is positioned, it is important to make sure the card is clearly visible to the guest.

Bells

Bone china bells are a fun addition to any tea party, and they work particularly well when you have a helper serving tea to your guests.

In this instance, your guests can ring for more tea when they are ready and your server doesn't have to guess when one of your guests needs more service. For a table of six to eight guests, two bells are usually sufficient, placed at either end of the table.

Buffet Tea

This form of service is often used when there are a larger number of guests at your tea and you may not have the table space to seat them. Or, it may just be the preferred way to showcase your tea.

Whatever the choice for a buffet tea, you will first need to decide on where the service area will be located. A dining room table or kitchen island are popular choices, or you could use a sideboard made specifically for the purpose.

Wherever the buffet is to be, it is important to make sure it is easily accessible to your guests. Ideally, they should be able to begin at one end, help themselves to the food, leave with their plate, cup and saucer and find a comfy place to sit – all without bumping into each other! So, consider the traffic flow and choose the best location.

The table set up is very similar to that of a seated tea, except there are no chairs around the table, and there are no designated place settings. If a table is used for the buffet, then it should have the same kinds of linens and over cloths as a sit-down tea. If the buffet is to be on a kitchen island, it really depends on the attractiveness of the island. Some granite worktops, for example, can look splendid unadorned, while other surfaces may benefit from a small lace cloth or similar covering. It all depends on what you have to work with. If you are in doubt, you should probably cover it in a pretty cloth.

The three-tiered plate stands (or similar presentation pieces) containing the food items, should be displayed with some decorative centerpieces placed between them. Small plates are positioned at the beginning of the buffet, while the cups and saucers will be the last items the guest picks up, and should be placed at the end. Folded napkins are placed at a convenient location on the table. Alternatively, they could be placed with the condiments.

Utensils will comprise of a knife and teaspoon for each guest. The knives can be either neatly laid out or placed in a basket or teapot (lined with a napkin). The small teaspoons can go directly on to the saucer with the cup. Your guests will have their hands full as it is, and will thank you for this added detail which has been taken care of for them. Serving tongs should be placed at the base of the three-tiered plate stands for those who wish to

use them. Even though the food is essentially "finger food", guests often prefer to pick up a sandwich with tongs rather than their fingers.

Condiments such as milk, lemons, sugar cubes and various spreads for the scones are placed in strategic places around the home, but close to where your guest are likely to sit. The guests will then simply help themselves when needed.

The Service of Tea

The service of tea can be handled in different ways, although it is preferable that your guests do not help themselves. There are a couple of reasons for this:

Firstly, and most importantly, is safety. The teapot can be very heavy and if made correctly, will be very hot. Consequently, if a guest should misjudge the weight or style of your teapot, any number of accidents could occur and this is the last thing you would wish to happen at your gathering. Secondly, because they are your guests they will probably expect you or someone assigned by you to play "mum" and serve the tea to them. It is the act of a gracious host to take care of her friends whilst in her home.

The best way is for a designated person, preferably one familiar with making and serving tea, to serve this beverage to your guests. If not using a professional, then certainly select someone who can follow direction and knows how to hold the pot correctly so as not to spill or drip on your carpet, your best table, or worse still, your guests.

It is advisable to remember some important pointers when serving hot tea. Always hold the pot with two hands; one on the handle and the other supporting the weight, just under the spout. To avoid burns and spills, use two napkins where your hands are positioned. The handle can get very hot and a napkin will protect your serving hand, while the other napkin can catch any errant drips. When pouring tea, etiquette dictates that the cup remain in its saucer on the table. In other words, do not remove the cup, add the tea and then replace it back on the table. Also, please remember to leave room in the cup for the addition of milk and/or lemon. It is only proper to fill the cup completely if a particular guest indicates it be served that way.

In a buffet situation when guests are milling around, never come up behind someone unannounced with a hot pot of tea in your hand! Your guest may be engrossed in deep conversation and not be aware you are there. Consequently, he or she could make an unexpected gesture with their arms, knocking the pot clean out of your hands!

The same applies if the guest is seated and you are serving. Always announce clearly that you are behind them and that you have hot tea. Even a brief touch of a hot teapot on a bare arm can cause all kinds of catastrophes and should be avoided at all costs.

And it really needs to be emphasized that whoever is serving any hot beverage should be especially careful around elderly guests, those with special needs, or children.

If these simple, yet important points are followed when serving tea, either seated or buffet style, your party will be remembered for the good time that was enjoyed by all.

CHAPTER FOUR
Menu

Food Preparation and Presentation

One of the most important components of your afternoon tea, apart from the tea of course, is going to be the food. It is worth taking the extra time to make sure the sandwiches are dainty and the desserts, delicate. This might sound like a daunting task, but is entirely possible, if you remember some important guidelines.

- Plan, plan and then plan some more
- Keep it simple
- Always begin with the freshest of ingredients
- Consider variety, taste, color and appearance
- Practice proper sanitation throughout food preparation

Plan, plan and then plan some more

You can never plan enough. I am a strong believer in lists, and have one going all the time when preparing for a party. Try to organize yourself as much as possible. My most valuable tool is a check sheet of my most common tea tasks. I begin by circling all that apply and then proceed to check off each task as it is completed.

Keep it simple

If this is your first attempt at putting on a tea party, make your choices simple, yet elegant. Try not to emulate the 5-star hotel downtown, which lavishes its guests with an afternoon tea fit for the Queen. Your tea can be every bit as stylish and enjoyable as long as you don't take on more than you can comfortably handle. Remember, this is a fun get together for your friends, and with a little help from this book, I am sure they will be duly impressed by what you can achieve.

Always begin with the freshest of ingredients

Whatever food items you choose to create, make sure you begin with the freshest of ingredients. Look for fruits and vegetables that are perfectly ripe – nothing too hard or too soft, and check the sell-by dates on other items. Fresh bread is essential and it is worth checking out a bakery which can provide you with the variety you need. Quality is of the utmost importance if you wish your tea items to turn out the way they are supposed to, and it's worth taking the extra time to pick out the best and most affordable within your budget.

Consider variety, taste, color and appearance

When presenting food, it is important to offer a variety of shapes, tastes, and colors on the plate. Even a peanut butter and jelly sandwich, cut into cute shapes with a cookie cutter will add interest and appeal. And when food items appeal to the eye, they usually will appeal to the taste buds too. Be sure to add a variety of food items to accommodate all of your guests' tastes and include at least one vegetarian option. Color is very visual and necessary on your plate presentations. On the dessert plate, for example, include a couple of red items (strawberries, raspberries, etc.) to really have your items stand out attractively.

Practice proper sanitation throughout food preparation

The health inspector isn't going to come knocking on your door to check on your sanitation practices, but it makes good sense to follow some simple guidelines in order to serve up a meal safely for yourself and your guests. Always wash your hands before handling food and use clean, sanitized utensils on a clean and sanitized work area. Be especially careful when handling raw chicken or any meats, and never allow them to come into contact with cooked or prepared foods. In other words, if you have just cut raw chicken on a cutting board, don't use the same board (without thoroughly cleaning it in hot, soapy water), for the cheese you need to grate for your sandwiches.

Tea Sandwiches

Afternoon tea just wouldn't be afternoon tea without an abundance of dainty finger sandwiches, and you really only need to offer a variety of two or three kinds to make your tea a special time.

Firstly, choose the freshest bread you can find and buy it as close to the date of your tea party as possible. Check the sell-by date on the bag by delving into the bread at the back of the shelf. If the store has been displaying their goods correctly, the newest arrivals will be behind the older ones. Look for a loaf that has thin to medium thick slices. Otherwise, your sandwich bread will overwhelm the filling.

When using three different sandwich fillings, offer three different types of bread. I particularly like whole wheat, 12-grain and oat nut breads, but there are lots to choose from at your local grocery store or bakery, and you need to taste different types to determine your own favorites.

Once the bread has been decided upon, you'll need to choose some different fillings. Your sandwich fillings can be anything that you like, even ones that you would normally find in your favorite deli or restaurant sandwiches. The only difference would be the amount of filling used. Tea sandwiches need to be finger size and delicate, not over-stuffed and spilling out on to the plate.

Some common tea sandwiches are egg, chicken, tuna or shrimp salad, thinly sliced roast beef with horseradish, sliced turkey with cheese, smoked salmon with pesto, cheese and chutney, and of course, that quintessential of all English tea sandwiches, cucumber dill.

Cucumber Dill Sandwich

8 slices oat nut bread
24 very thin slices of English cucumber (unpeeled)
1 tablespoon of malt vinegar
1 teaspoon of sea salt
4 tablespoon butter, softened for spreading

Cream Cheese Dill Mixture (enough to make 6-8 sandwiches)
8 oz package regular cream cheese
1 tablespoon fresh chopped dill (or teaspoon dried dill weed)
1 tablespoon dried minced onion flakes
½ teaspoon lemon pepper seasoning

Method:

    Mix all the ingredients for the cream cheese mixture in a large bowl until light and spreadable. Refrigerate until needed. Cut the cucumber slices so thinly you are almost able to see through them. Place in a colander with a plate underneath. Sprinkle with the vinegar and salt. Toss lightly. Cover with a paper towel and press down. Leave in a cool place to drain for 30 minutes. Remove the cucumber slices and place on a dry paper towel. Pat dry any moisture still left on the cucumber.

    To assemble, butter each slice of bread lightly. Take about a teaspoon of the cream cheese mixture and spread it on the bread. Lay six slightly overlapping slices of the cucumber on one side of the bread. Pat dry again and then place the remaining buttered bread on top. Stack the sandwiches, secure tightly in plastic wrap and store in the refrigerator until ready for service.

Makes 4 whole sandwiches or 16 finger sandwiches.

Curried Egg Salad

8 slices of whole wheat bread
Butter, softened for spreading
4 eggs, hard boiled, shelled and chopped
½ teaspoon curry powder
½ teaspoon salt
1 tablespoon fresh chives (or ½ teaspoon dried)
3-4 tablespoons (approximately) mayonnaise to mix

Method:

Mix together the eggs, curry powder, salt and chives and add enough mayonnaise to moisten. The consistency should be neither too dry nor too wet. Taste and adjust seasonings if necessary. Cover and refrigerate until needed.

Butter the bread slices lightly. Divide the mixture on to half of the bread slices. Top with the remaining slices. Stack together and then secure tightly in plastic wrap until ready for service.

Makes 4 whole sandwiches or 16 finger sandwiches.

Note: All bread, no matter what the filling, should be lightly buttered first. This layer of fat helps protect the bread from a moist filling and therefore helps to prevent sogginess.

Turkey and Boursin Cheese Pinwheel

You will need freshly baked pumpernickel bread (or bread of your choice), cut lengthways (your baker must do this for you), so that you are able to roll up this sandwich. Depending on the size of the loaf, you should get about seven long slices this way.

7 thin slices of deli-style turkey
7 slices of pumpernickel bread, cut lengthways
Butter, softened for spreading

Boursin cheese spread:
1 – 5oz packet of Boursin Cheese
2 tablespoons mayonnaise

Method:

Gently break apart the cheese with a fork. Add mayonnaise, plus a little more if necessary, to form a spreading consistency. Cover and refrigerate until needed.

Remove the crusts from the short ends of the bread. Lay the slices with the length away from you. Lightly butter each piece. Spread about two tablespoons of the cheese mixture over the bread. Lay a slice of turkey on top of the cheese and then roll up, jelly-roll fashion. Wrap tightly in plastic wrap and refrigerate for at least four hours or overnight. Repeat with the other slices. When ready to serve, remove plastic and cut off the end. Discard. Cut the roll into 4 or 5 slices. Keep them covered. (See Keeping your Sandwiches Fresh).

Makes 7 rolled pinwheels or 28-35 slices.

How many sandwiches to make?

If you've invited six guests to your tea party, but are unsure of how many sandwiches to serve, there is an easy way to work it out.

It is better to have too much than too little, so allow for two whole sandwiches per person. This equates to eight finger sandwiches each, since most sandwiches are cut into four tea size pieces. So, let's say you have chosen three types of sandwiches: egg salad, cucumber dill, and turkey and Boursin cheese pinwheels.

Six guests x two sandwiches = twelve sandwiches

Twelve sandwiches divided by
three sandwich choices   =   Four whole sandwiches
of each variety

This will provide you with forty-eight finger sandwiches
– each of your guests receiving eight pieces per person.

When you are ready to plate your sandwiches, gather together the following items:

- A serving platter or plate lined with a pretty doily
- A piece of wax paper large enough to cover the serving platter
- A moistened paper towel to go over the wax paper
- Plastic wrap (if planning to hold the plated sandwiches for a few hours)

Cutting your Sandwiches

First of all, you will need to cut off the crusts of your sandwiches. Tea sandwiches are delicate and I'm afraid, crusts are not allowed!

Stack three or four sandwiches together. Using a very sharp, serrated knife, slice down each side of the stack, being careful to only cut off the brown crust. It would be boring to have all of your sandwiches look the same way, so try to use different shapes to add interest to your plate. For example, you could cut one stack of similar sandwiches into four fingers, another stack into triangles by cutting an "X" across, and another stack into squares. The pinwheel type of sandwich roll will yield round sandwiches.

Plating your Sandwiches

Beautifully made and cut sandwiches can look sloppy if just thrown on a plate. They deserve to be presented well. Think of your serving plate as an artist's canvas. It needs to be balanced in appearance, color and texture, with the food placed in such a way so as to please the eye. This is why there should be different shapes, different types of breads, and different fillings for your sandwiches.

Using the three different types of sandwiches discussed, I have illustrated how you could possibly arrange them. For the purpose of this explanation, the egg salad sandwiches have been cut into fingers, the cucumber dill have been cut into squares, and the pinwheels have been sliced into round sandwiches.

diagram 1

It is important not to overload the plate. You can comfortably place 24 assorted finger sandwiches on one 10" plate, with an allowance for the doily edge to show. It is a good idea to keep the same type of sandwich together in one or two places on the plate. For instance, half of the egg salad could be placed on one side of the plate with the remaining placed on the opposite side. If you do decide to split up this one sandwich, you should also split another type to balance out the look. So, the square cucumber could be placed on the remaining opposite sides of the plate. The pinwheels then could be placed all together in the middle. (see diagram1)

Alternatively, all of the egg salad could be placed in the center of the plate, with the cucumber split up and the pinwheels tucked in between. (see diagram 2)

Try to take into consideration the color and texture of the bread. For example, the darkness of the pumpernickel looks good next to the contrast of a lighter colored bread, like the oat nut.

With our fictional six-guest tea party, I would suggest using two separate serving platters, or three-tiered plate stands. On an average dining room table, this will ensure your guests won't have to stretch in order to reach the food.

diagram 2

Keeping your Sandwiches Fresh

Place the wax paper over the sandwiches. Carefully lay the moistened paper towel on top of the wax paper. If using, tightly seal the plate with plastic wrap and store in the refrigerator. The duo of wax paper and dampened paper towel really helps to keep the sandwiches moist and fresh without allowing them to go soggy. The plastic wrap cuts out air and ensures that the paper towel stays moist. Your sandwiches will remain fresh and soft until time of service.

Scones

The original scone is said to have come from Scotland, and is named for the Stone of Destiny, where Scottish kings were formally crowned. Back then, around 1505, this first scone contained mainly oats and was cooked on a griddle. It has changed a lot over the years and is now usually made with flour, butter, sugar, added fruit and then baked in the oven.

It can be found in rounds, triangles and diamonds, but no matter the shape, one question persists – does the word scone rhyme with cone or con? It all depends on where you live in the British Isles, since the northerners tend to rhyme it with con and the southerners with cone. Either way is acceptable as long as the finished product tastes good!

Scones are an essential part of an afternoon tea. Your guests will expect to find them on your tea table along with such glorious accompaniments as Devonshire cream, strawberry jam and lemon curd to lavish all over them.

There are numerous recipes for scones; some containing fruit, some just plain; some even containing chocolate chips! It's all a matter of taste and preference and your choice should be whatever you think your guests might like. If you're not sure, offer a couple of varieties.

This recipe comes from the Dorchester Hotel in London.

Tea Scones

3 cups cake flour
3 teaspoons baking powder
1/3 rd cup butter, cut into small pieces
2 eggs, whisked
¼ cup sugar
¾ cup milk
2 tablespoons milk for brushing tops
　of scones
Sugar for sprinkling on top of scones

Mix the flour, baking powder and butter together by hand to form breadcrumbs. Add eggs and mix quickly. Dissolve sugar in milk and add to the flour mix in a steady stream. Mix for a minute. Do not overwork the dough.

Press out the dough to a 2" thickness and allow to relax for two minutes. Cut out the individual scones with a 2" cutter. Brush the tops with milk and sprinkle with sugar. Rest for one hour. Bake in a preheated oven at 300 degrees for 20 minutes. Makes approximately 15—20 scones.

Note: You may add ¾ cup of desired chopped fruit (golden raisins, candied cherries, dried apricots, blueberries, etc.) at the breadcrumb stage, before adding the eggs.

These scones can be made ahead and frozen before they are baked. Simply freeze until solid on a parchment paper lined baking sheet and then transfer the frozen scones to a zippered freezer bag, squeezing out the air. When ready to bake, remove from freezer, thaw to room temperature and follow recipe directions.

Devonshire Cream

Devonshire or "clotted" cream originates in the west counties of England, primarily Devon, Cornwall and Somerset, and is a delicious cream containing approximately 58% butterfat content. It is a traditional accompaniment to scones and should be included on your tea table.

Don't be fooled into believing those who say they make their own, because it can only really be made if you own a Jersey or Guernsey cow! These breeds of cow are known to produce an already rich milk, and benefit further by feeding from the lush green grass in the southwest portions of these counties in the English countryside.

The milk that is used has to be straight from the cow and is therefore unpasteurized. It is then heated, very gently, for several hours until a thick layer of yellowy cream rises to the top. This is then skimmed off and sold as clotted or Devonshire cream, depending on which county it comes from.

To my knowledge, the cream in this natural form is not readily available in the United States. However, you can purchase the next best thing – a pasteurized version of real Devonshire cream. It is sold by the Devon Cream Company and can be found in many upscale grocery stores or online. This is the Devonshire cream I use at my teas.

Lemon Curd

You can purchase lemon curd from the majority of grocery stores these days, but there is nothing like homemade lemon curd, and it really is very easy to make yourself. If you have a little time, it is worth the effort and once you have tasted it, you'll never go back to store-bought again.

Grated rind and 7oz juice from 3 medium lemons
12 oz sugar
6 oz unsalted butter
3 eggs, beaten

Grate rind and squeeze juice from the lemons (use extra if needed to produce 7 oz of juice). Place in a double boiler (or pan over simmering water), with the sugar. Stir until the sugar is dissolved. Add the cut up butter and whisked eggs and stir continuously until the mixture thickens (about 30 minutes). Strain through a sieve into sterilized containers and seal. The lemon curd will keep in the refrigerator for about three weeks.

Lemon curd, Devonshire cream and Strawberry jam

Pastries

The crowning glories of your tea, so to speak, are all the wonderful pastries that are so pleasing to the eye and so tempting to the taste buds.

Plan to serve at least four different kinds of pastries. You can, of course, include more depending on your time or budget, but four types will look nice on the plate as well as offer your guests a choice.

You can, of course, spend hours fiddling with little bits of chocolate cut into intricate shapes, or make garnishes that you can't even pronounce. But who needs to go to all that trouble? With minimum effort, you should be able to produce perfectly attractive pastries that look great and taste wonderful.

Some of my favorites include chocolate-dipped strawberries, key lime tartlets, brownie sundaes and teapot shortbreads. These four would work well because they offer a variety of shapes, textures, flavors and colors. If you find your pastry plate contains too many desserts of a bland similar color, add a splash of red, either with strawberries or raspberries and your plate will liven up immediately.

The pastries I mentioned are all reasonably easy to make, but if you really don't have the time or inclination to bake and you want to purchase all of your pastries from your favorite pastry shop, this is absolutely fine. It's important to remember that your guests are there to enjoy your company and the company of your other guests. Food is important, of course, but it's secondary to the gathering of special friends in your home who are there for the company and conversation.

Chocolate-dipped Strawberries

12 firm, ripe, unblemished strawberries (look for ones with fresh green tops and if possible, ones of similar size)
8 oz good quality chocolate (either milk or dark)
2 oz white chocolate
Wax paper sheet and wooden skewers

Method

Wipe the strawberries with a moistened paper towel and place on a dry paper towel. Remove any brownish leaves. In a double boiler, or in a bowl over gently simmering water, place the broken or chopped milk or dark chocolate and stir until smooth and melted. Do not let the water get too hot. Remove the bowl from the heat, but save the hot water.

Take a wooden skewer and gently push it into the top of the strawberry until you are able to secure a good hold on to it. Dip the strawberry about three-quarters of the way into the chocolate, allowing the excess to drip off into the bowl. Place on a wax sheet to dry. Continue with the remaining strawberries. You can place the finished strawberries into the refrigerator for a few minutes to hurry this process along.

While they are drying, place the broken white chocolate into another small bowl and place over the simmering water. Stir until it has melted and become smooth. Remove the dried chocolate strawberries from the refrigerator. With the tip of spoon, drizzle random lines back and forth across the strawberry with the white chocolate. It really doesn't matter what design you use; it will all look very professional!

Place into pretty paper cases and keep refrigerated until ready to serve. This amount will allow for two strawberries per person, based on our tea for six guests.

Teapot Shortbread

4 oz unsalted butter
2 oz sugar
4 oz all-purpose flour
2 oz ground rice flour
Pinch of salt

Method

Heat the oven to 375 F. Line a baking tray with parchment paper.

Cream the butter and sugar together until light and fluffy. Sift the flours and salt together and gradually add to the butter mixture until well blended. Empty out on to a floured board and knead together with your hands until the mixture forms a ball.

On a floured work surface, roll out to about a ¼" thickness. Using a cutter of your choice (I use a teapot, but any shape will work), cut out shortbread and place on a baking sheet. Bake for about 8-10 minutes or until just starting to turn golden brown at the edges.

Cool and keep in an airtight container. Freezes very well. Makes about 20-25 teapots, but amounts will vary depending on what size cutter you use.

Brownie Sundaes

Your favorite brownie recipe
(either homemade or box mix)
Sweetened whipped cream
Candied cherries
Colored sprinkles

Method

Make and bake the brownies, using a pan which will yield approximately 1" thick brownies. Cut into 1" wide strips and then cut those strips into diamond shapes by cutting on an angle every 1".

Pipe a whipped cream rosette on each brownie, top with a ½ candied cherry and toss a few sprinkles over the entire pastry to finish it off. Place in decorative paper cases.

Key Lime Tartlets

Pastry:
9 oz pastry or cake flour
7 oz unsalted butter, cut into pieces
1 teaspoon salt
1 egg, whisked
1 tablespoon milk

Key Lime Mix:
1/3 rd cup Key Lime juice
1 – 14 oz can sweetened condensed milk
3 egg yolks, mixed
Sweetened, whipped cream & lime zest

Method:

Make the pastry in a food processor if possible. Sift flour and salt into the bowl. Add butter and pulse until well mixed. Mix egg and milk together. With the machine running, add the egg and milk until the mixture comes together. Empty into a bowl and knead until smooth. Cover and rest the dough in the refrigerator for 20 minutes.

If making this by hand, take a large mixing bowl and sift the flour and salt. Add the small pieces of butter and mix until fine breadcrumbs are formed. Add the egg and milk and work the dough until smooth. Refrigerate and rest for 20 minutes.

Working with a piece of the dough, roll it out to about ¼" in depth. Spray the mini-muffin pan with vegetable oil spray or a little butter. Using a 2" cutter, or a cutter to fit your size pan, cut out required circles. Place in the pan and crimp the edges. Chill.

Make the key lime mix by whisking together the juice, condensed milk and egg yolks. Set aside. Whip the cream and add enough powdered sugar to sweeten. Pre-bake the pastry shells for approximately 8-10 minutes in a 350 degree oven. They should still retain a light color.

When cool, add a teaspoon of key lime mix into each of the shells. Pop back in the oven for about 12 minutes. When completely cooled, place carefully in a paper case, pipe a rosette of whipped cream on each tartlet and garnish with a little grated lime zest.

Note: Any leftover key lime mix can be frozen for later use. Be sure to use an airtight, plastic container.

CHAPTER FIVE
Tea

Tea is obviously the heart and soul of a tea party and without it, your get-together wouldn't exist. But where does this simple beverage start its life?

No matter if the tea is green, oolong or of the black variety, tea all comes from the same plant – the Camellia Sinensis. This tea bush grows in sub-tropical and higher tropical elevations around the equator, and the top producing countries are India, China, Sri Lanka and Kenya. Like fine wine, the tea bush is affected by soil, elevation, moisture and heat. Consequently, optimum conditions will produce optimum tea leaves.

Cultivating the tea is a very laborious affair, since only the top two leaves and a bud are picked, usually by hand. It takes at least 4 ½ pounds of freshly picked leaves to make one pound of black tea.

The four main types of tea are white, green, oolong and black. Even though they all come from the same genetic variety of plant, it is what happens to the leaves after they are picked that decides which kind of tea it will become.

White and green teas are processed very little and are considered unfermented. Oolong tea undergoes a short time of oxidation and is considered semi-fermented, and black tea, on the other hand, is completely fermented, hence its dark color. The more fermentation, the more caffeine is present in the tea.

Choice of Tea

So what kind of tea to serve? Even with so many different varieties to choose from, this is not a difficult task. You probably have a favorite brew already, or know of a particular kind your guests like, which will make your job easy. But if not, keep it simple and pick just a couple of types, plus a decaffeinated offering and your guests will be very happy.

I would suggest choosing one plain tea like English Breakfast, Assam or Darjeeling, (noting that English Breakfast is a stronger black tea than Darjeeling, and Assam is somewhere in between), one flavored tea like an Earl Grey or a fruited black tea, and one decaffeinated of your choice.

Herbal teas, incidentally, contain no actual tea leaves and therefore, no caffeine. They are made up entirely of stems, flowers, roots and buds of plants and are not, therefore, a true tea.

How to Make a Proper Pot of Tea

Making the perfect pot of brewed tea isn't difficult if you follow a few simple steps:

1. Always start with fresh, cold water.
2. Bring the kettle to a boil and warm the tea pot (heavy ceramic or silver is best), by swishing around the hot liquid and then discarding it.
3. If using loose leaf tea, measure out the desired amount into a tea ball or tea infuser. It is best to experiment with your choice of tea leaves to ensure you reach the desired brew strength. An average strength would be achieved by using 1-2 heaping teaspoons per 4-cup pot, but different teas do produce different results. If using tea bags, 2 tea bags for the same size pot are usually sufficient.
4. Bring the kettle to a rolling boil (one which is energetic and bubbling furiously), and pour over the tea ball or tea bags in the pot. This is required for all black teas, whereas green teas prefer an infusion from water just under the boil.
5. Cover the pot with a tea cozy (or folded tea towel), and allow to steep for at least 3-5 minutes. If after 3 full minutes, your tea is too strong, you have placed too much tea in the tea ball. If it is too weak, you will need to adjust the amount. Whichever strength you would like, it is important to always brew for the full time for maximum release of flavor from the tea. Note: Some teas take longer to infuse than others. Darjeeling, for instance, needs the full 5 minutes of steeping time.
6. Remove the tea ball or tea bags and discard the leaves. (Great for the compost). Rinse and refill the tea ball or unwrap your tea bags ready for the next pot of tea.
7. Cover the pot with the tea cozy until ready for service.
8. Always serve your tea piping hot and fresh. There is nothing worse than tepid or stale tea.

Note: If you don't have a tea ball or infuser you can certainly make good tea without one. The tea would need to be poured into the cup through a tea strainer. The only problem with this method is the possibility of the tea becoming "stewed" and bitter if the leaves are left too long in the teapot.

Tea Cozies

Tea cozies are simply hats for teapots. Made out of a variety of materials, cozies have liners of thick batting which helps retain the heat of the tea in the pot. They are generally available online or from tea specialty stores, or you could make your own. Patterns can be found at your favorite fabric shop.

Tea Accompaniments

Along with tea, the gracious host should also offer a small dish of cut lemons, sugar cubes and a pitcher of milk. These three items are usually found sitting together on the tea table, or in the case of a buffet, placed in several rooms.

The lemon pieces do not need to be very large. First cut the lemon into several ¼" thick slices. Then cut each slice into four (or just in half if the lemon is small). Place these in a decorative container – a small glass or ceramic bowl is fine, or even on a decorative plate. You will need to put a tiny fork with the lemons for ease of service.

If you don't have decorated sugar cubes, don't worry. Plain sugar cubes or even regular granulated sugar is fine to use. Just add a delicate pair of sugar tongs or a small teaspoon, if using regular sugar.

Sugar cubes are easily decorated, if you have a little time. They can be as simple as attaching individual floral sprinkles (available in the baking aisle) with a dab of royal icing. Or, alternatively you could hand-pipe delicate designs of your choice. If you have ever decorated a cake, you should be able to decorate a few sugar cubes with no problem. They are fun to do and your guests will be in awe of your hidden talents!

Milk should always be offered for those guests who like tea taken that way. I find that 2% milk is the best choice for tea. Anything less is too weak and whole milk is too creamy and overpowering. 2% is just right.

A Little Tea History

The origin of tea goes back to 2737 BC when a legendary Chinese Emperor by the name of Shen Nung was said to have discovered tea while traveling across his native country.

As a scientist and believer in strict hygiene, he would always insist on boiling his drinking water. Legend has it that one day, when his servants were duly following his orders, a few leaves blew down from a nearby tree, infusing the water a golden color. Shen Nung was so intrigued by this happening that he tasted the brew and liked it. And so, they say, the rest is history.

Buddhist monks quickly spread the news of this newly discovered beverage throughout China. Later, seeds for cultivation were taken to Japan by a monk called Dengyo Daishi. As the tea plant grew and thrived, so did its popularity. Green tea was the tea of choice in both China and Japan and still is to this day. In Japan, tea was incorporated over many hundreds of years into a very complex ceremony known as the Japanese Tea Ceremony. During the ceremony, which can last up to four hours, guests and hosts alike are searching for peace, harmony, respect, purity and tranquility between themselves and the universe. A special room is designated for this unique experience.

Tea and Europe

It is thought that Dutch traders first introduced tea into Europe in the 17th Century. Its popularity continued and spread into Italy, France, Germany and Portugal. But, the interest was short-lived in Germany and France where coffee became the beverage of choice. It was around 1658 when tea first made itself known in England. It was hailed as a special liquid that could cure all kinds of ills, from simple headaches to scurvy!

When King Charles II married Catherine of Braganza, a Portuguese princess, part of her dowry was a chest of China tea. She was known to be very fond of tea and started to serve it in the royal court, and its popularity spread even more. Unfortunately, since tea was highly taxed (equivalent to $1.20-$4.50 a pound in today's market) only the very rich could afford to enjoy it. Tea leaves were locked away like jewels in a caddy and only the lady of the house would be permitted to hold the key, dispensing small amounts as required. Oftentimes, the leaves would be used three or four times, and then be given to the servants. Once the final drop of tea was tasted by the staff, the spent leaves would yet again be sold out the back door for a penny. The commodity was certainly not wasted!

Tea and America

In 1765, Britain's Stamp Act, followed in 1767 by the Townsend Act, placed heavy taxes on various commodities in the colonies, including one of their favorites, tea. Since the colonists had no representation in English parliament, they protested these high taxes. Britain responded by retracting some taxes, with one exception – a high duty on tea. The British government knew that this showed their power and control over the colonies. But the colonists weren't deterred. They found ways to smuggle their tea in from Holland, proving very lucrative for the smugglers but upsetting the English importers, the East India Company.

The East India Company who imported the tea, soon found themselves with a surplus of tea and profits dwindling. To help them out and to keep some control over the colonies, Parliament gave the East India Company total monopoly on tea imported to America and reduced the duty. The colonists weren't fooled by this plan. They realized that even though they'd be paying very little for their tea, they would also, by their actions, be admitting to the mother country that Parliament had a right to tax them.

This move angered the smugglers who lost out on their business, and the colonists who saw the move as another way to manipulate them. So, in December of 1773, when three ships arrived in Boston Harbor, it was decided by almost 7,000 very angry locals that they should be turned away without payment of the duty. A message was taken to the customs collector, but he refused to let the ships leave saying the duty should be paid to them. When these local men heard the response from the customs collector, they took matters into their own hands. They dressed as native Indians, secretly climbed aboard the ships and threw the entire cargo of tea into Boston's famed harbor in protest.

The Boston Tea Party, as it was known, laid the groundwork for the beginning of the War of Independence which in turn, gave way to an independent America in 1776.

The Beginning of Afternoon Tea

It wasn't until much later, in 1840, that Anna, Duchess of Bedford unwittingly created the gentle pastime known as Afternoon Tea.

In those days, breakfast was usually served early in the day with little or no lunch offered midday and dinner following many hours later. She found she needed something to calm the "sinking feeling" she would experience between these meals, usually around 4pm. So, at her request, her servants would bring her a small sandwich, some sweetmeats and hot tea in the late afternoon, all served on the finest of china, with tea poured from a silver pot.

She so enjoyed this mid-afternoon respite that she wanted to share it with her closest of friends. Soon, the social elite of the day spread the word of this new relaxing activity and afternoon tea was born. Today, we are enjoying a rebirth of this wonderful experience as more and more ladies (and gentlemen) are partaking in afternoon tea, both in their homes and in the finest of hotels.

CHAPTER SIX
Children's Tea Parties

A tea party for young ones can be such an exciting time, especially if their friends and stuffed animals can join in the fun too.

Encourage the child to participate as much as possible in the planning of the party. Children have specific ideas on what they would like included and some of their choices can be very helpful to you.

If possible, provide a box of dress-up goodies and let the imaginations flow. Dressing up is always a special treat and children love to be "just like the grown-ups" by wearing oversized hats, clip-clop shoes and glittery costume jewelry. Even little boys can get in on the act by wearing a smart jacket and tie and maybe even a hat and white silk scarf!

`Oftentimes, noisy, active children, dressed up in their parent's or grandparent's finery will turn into perfectly mannered young people once seated at a tea table. It's as if, miraculously, they knew all along how to behave! However, when things don't go exactly to plan, a little etiquette lesson can go a long way and can certainly do no harm.

You have a captive audience. With a setting as enjoyable as afternoon tea, they will not even realize they are learning something valuable. Show them what a napkin is used for and what <u>not</u> to do with it. Teach them how to hold the utensils properly, how not to speak with their mouths full and how to talk to each other in their "library" voices. Teach them how to carefully pass items around the table and how to ask politely if they should need something. Proper manners are tools every person should be encouraged to use on an everyday basis, no matter what the age.

Party Ideas

Children are renowned finicky eaters, so it is important to provide some commonly liked foods. The key here is to take ordinary food and change it into something magical. Although not absolutely necessary, choosing a theme for your child's party will help you to organize the menu. For example, if your child has a favorite teddy bear, an easy tea party would be a version of a "teddy bear's picnic". Cookies cut out as teddy bears, picnic foods in miniature, a red and white checked tablecloth, and of course, lots of teddy bears in attendance.

Perhaps your young person wishes to be the Queen and wants to invite all of her ladies-in-waiting for an afternoon tea. Crowns could be made and decorated (a large one for the Queen of course), and some simple cloaks made from material oddments. The tea table should be set with lots of glitz and glitter befitting a royal gathering, using sequins or confetti, and the tea can be served in a real teapot, but actually be apple juice or lemonade and announced as "palace tea". Provide some favorite sandwich fixings in fancy shapes and maybe some cut up fruit "jewels" . . . . well, you get the idea.

The important thing to remember is that the children are having fun actually learning how to behave, as well as using their imagination at the same time. With a little effort on your part, your child's tea party will be one fondly remembered by all who attend; a cherished memory that will stay with them into their adult years.

CHAPTER SEVEN
Frequently Asked Questions

Is there really an Earl of Sandwich?

Yes, and the sandwich was really named after him. The story goes that in 1762, John Montagu, the 4th Earl of Sandwich, was gambling at cards. Becoming hungry, he didn't want to leave the table since he was winning, so he sent his servant for two of his favorite foods, bread and meat. The servant came back with the meat sandwiched between the bread and so, they say, the first sandwich was created. Incidentally, the Earl won the equivalent of $10,000 that day!

What time should Afternoon Tea be served?

Whatever time you wish. Although traditionally it was served between 3-4 p.m., when Anna, the 7th Duchess of Bedford experienced a "sinking feeling" between an early breakfast, light lunch and very late dinner. For today's purposes, anytime after noontime is considered acceptable.

What is the difference between Afternoon Tea and High Tea?

Afternoon tea is about everything elegant, and is also known as low tea because of the coffee type of table that is sometimes used. Served generally between 3—4 p.m. the meal consists of dainty sandwiches, scones with Devonshire cream and jam, followed by delicate pastries. The table is covered with fine lace and is resplendent with fresh flowers, bone china cups and a sparkling silver teapot. It is a time to dress in your best and engage in some refined conversation. It's about relaxing in a quiet place and taking time to reflect on the importance of friendship in life.

High tea, on the other hand, is totally different and occurs around supper time. It represents a heartier fare and is associated originally with the north country of England, where hard-working family members, after hours of working in the fields and factories, would arrive home expecting a satisfying meal. The large farmhouse table (of regular height, hence the name high tea), still served tea, but not from a silver teapot into a bone china cup. The pot would be large and plain and the china simple and sturdy. There is nothing delicate about this meal. Food items could include hearty soups, meat pies, hunks of cheese, wholesome breads and favorite desserts. The conversation would be lively and noisy, typical of family members discussing their busy day.

Should you have your pinky in or out?

Definitely in! Before handles were added to cups, ladies had a difficult time holding the hot bowl-style tea cup, so would stick their fingers out to avoid the discomfort. Today, this mannerism is thought to be snobbish.

Milk in first or last?

This is all a matter of preference. When bone china was first introduced, it was very fragile. It was thought that the hot tea would crack the delicate cups, so milk was added first to temper the hot liquid. Nowadays, cups are sturdier and the tempering is not necessary. If you know the strength of the tea, put the milk in first. If you are not sure, add the milk after to achieve the desired strength. I believe Queen Elizabeth II adds her milk last.

What is Royal Tea?

It is all the regular offerings of afternoon tea with the addition of a glass of champagne or sherry for each guest.

Is there a proper dress code for Afternoon Tea?

There are those who really like to go to town and wear the flowing tea gown, large floppy hat and white gloves. But if you don't possess any of these items, your "Sunday best" will suffice. The aim is to be elegant, yet comfortable.

What is the proper procedure when using napkins?

Napkins are provided to you for the sole purpose of catching any crumbs, or for dabbing your mouth, should some food item end up on your chin. They are not for blowing your nose or waving about while having conversation.

Proper procedure when seated is to quietly unfold the napkin and place it across your lap. If you should need to leave the table during the tea, the napkin should be left on your chair, not on the table. Placing the napkin on the table indicates you have finished and should not be done until the host first places her napkin by the side of her plate.

What topics of conversation are acceptable at tea?

It is wise to keep the conversation light and non-confrontational. Stay away from politics, religion (unless the guests as a whole are a religious group), personal health issues and anything related to you and only you. For instance, you might be totally in awe of your little grandson's achievements from birth through high school, but too much information about this topic might not interest everyone else.

Is it really possible to decaffeinate regular caffeinated tea?

If you forget to buy decaffeinated tea for your guests, it is possible to remove 80-90% of the caffeine by doing it yourself. Simply pour boiling water over regular tea as normal. Steep for 30 seconds and then pour off the liquid. Add freshly boiled water to the same tea leaves and brew as normal.

How long can I keep tea?

Loose leaf tea has a shelf life of approximately one year. It is important to keep tea away from natural enemies such as moisture, light, heat and strong odors. To help retain freshness, it should be kept in the original packaging and stored in an airtight container. Tea bags will begin to lose their flavors after six months, and should be treated in the same manner as loose leaf tea. Incidentally, no tea should ever be frozen.

I like the flavor of lemon and milk. Can I use both in tea?

You could, but you'd end up with an unsightly mess! The acid in the lemon will react with the milk and cause it to curdle, or separate. So choose either, but not at the same time.

Is tea really healthy for you?

Yes, it really is! Tea naturally contains antioxidants and vitamins, A, B, C, E and K. It also contains nutrients such as fluoride, manganese, zinc, potassium, iron, folic acid and niacin. Research indicates that the benefits of tea might also help to prevent certain cancers and heart disease.

Was Earl Grey a real person?

Yes, indeed. He was Charles Grey, 2nd Earl and a British Prime Minister from 1830-1834. The story goes that, while on a visit to China, a British diplomat saved the life of an emperor's son and in gratitude, a special blend of tea was named after the prime minister. The tea is flavored with oil of Bergamot which gives it a unique citrus aroma and flavor.

Who invented iced tea?

Iced tea was invented purely by chance. While at the St. Louis World's Fair in 1904, an Englishman by the name of Richard Blechynden was trying to sell his hot tea. As it was a sweltering day, he wasn't having much luck. In frustration, he finally poured all of his tea over ice to preserve it and then found it to be extremely favorable with the crowds. Iced tea has remained popular in America to this day.

What are "elevenses"?

This term in England refers to the time (11:00 a.m. or thereabouts), when work stops and a tea or coffee break is taken. The beverage is often accompanied by a sticky bun or biscuit (cookie), or similar confection.

What is the proper way to eat a scone?

It is easiest if it is sliced in half horizontally, but alternatively you could break it into bite-sized pieces and enjoy it that way. Spread with either jam or lemon curd and then top with a generous dollop of Devonshire cream. Yum!